Judicial Independence and the Federal Courts

by

Bruce Ragsdale

Director, Federal Judicial History Office
Federal Judicial Center

Federal Judicial Center
Federal Judicial History Office
2006

Contents

Introduction

This teaching module was developed by the Federal Judicial Center to support judges and court staff who want to speak to various groups about the history of an independent federal judiciary. It focuses on historical debates about judicial independence. Other modules in this series examine the constitutional origins of the judiciary and the development of the federal court system. Each module includes four components: background discussion to serve as talking points; a PowerPoint presentation that can be downloaded to provide a visual guide to the speaker's remarks; a list of suggested discussion topics; and selections from historical documents that can be used in discussion with the audience or incorporated in the speaker's remarks.

Part I. Judicial Independence and the Federal Courts— Talking Points

1. Constitutional Protections and Political Debates

A central principle of the United States system of government holds that judges should be able to reach decisions free from political pressure. The framers of the Constitution shared a commitment to judicial independence, and they organized the new government to ensure that federal judges would have a proper measure of independence from the executive and legislative branches. The Constitution guaranteed that judges would serve "during good behavior" and would be protected from any reduction in their salaries, thus preventing removal by a President who opposed their judicial philosophy and congressional retaliation against unpopular decisions. These twin foundations of judicial independence were well established in the British judicial system of the eighteenth century and had been enacted by many of the new state constitutions following independence from Great Britain. But the constitutional outline for the judiciary also ensured that the court system would always be subject to the political process and thus to popular expectations. The Constitution's provision for "such inferior courts as the Congress may from time to time ordain and establish," granted the legislative branch the most powerful voice in deciding the structure and jurisdiction of the nation's court system. The appointment of judges by the President, with the advice and consent of the Senate, further ensured that important aspects of the judiciary would be part of the political process. The inherent tension between provisions for judicial independence and the

1

elected branches' authority to define the court system has led to recurring debates on judicial tenure and the federal courts' jurisdiction.

Throughout United States history, unpopular court decisions and the general authority of the federal judiciary have prompted calls to limit judges' terms of office, to define more narrowly the jurisdiction of the federal courts, or to limit judicial review—the courts' authority to determine the constitutionality of laws. Underlying the debates on judicial independence have been basic questions about the proper balance of Congress's authority to define the court system and the need to protect a judge's ability to reach decisions independent of political pressure. The debates have also addressed the extent to which the judiciary should be independent of popular opinion in a system of government where all power is based on the consent of the governed. Other debates have raised the need for safeguards for judicial independence in addition to those provided by the Constitution.

2.   Debates on the Constitution

The delegates to the Constitutional Convention accepted with little debate the provisions for service during good behavior and for protected salaries. Only during the ratification debates in the states did political writers more fully explore the Constitution's definition of judicial independence. The most famous commentary came in *The Federalist* essays of Alexander Hamilton, who argued that "the complete independence of the courts of justice is peculiarly essential in a limited Constitution," by which he meant a Constitution that placed limits on the authority of all government office-holders. The judiciary's responsibility, according to Hamilton, was to enforce the people's will as expressed in the Constitution and thus to prevent the abuse of power by the executive and especially the legislature. "Permanent tenure" was the most important foundation of the courts' role as "bulwarks . . . against legislative encroachments."

A prominent Anti-Federalist critic of the Constitution acknowledged the importance of judicial independence as secured by service during good behavior, but "Brutus" also recognized that the judicial independence envisioned by the Constitution was unprecedented. Judges would be removable only by impeachment and conviction of "high crimes and misdemeanors" rather than by a vote of the legislature, as was the case in most other governments with judicial tenure during good behavior. "Brutus" warned that regardless of errors of judgment or inability to carry out their duties, federal judges would be "independent of the people, of the legislature, and of every power under heaven." He also worried that these largely unaccountable judges would have the final say on the meaning of the Constitution, but Hamilton and other framers of the proposed government thought that the courts' responsibility to determine the constitutionality of laws, and thus to protect individual rights, was precisely the reason for the extraordinary protections of judicial independence. Hamilton dismissed concerns about unchecked judicial power, since the courts had "no influence over either the sword or the purse."

3. Political Parties and the Federal Courts

The framers' hopes for judicial independence were quickly challenged by the unexpected emergence of political parties in the 1790s. By the end of the decade, nominations of judges and any legislation relating to the courts became intertwined with the intense political struggle between Federalists and Republicans. After passage of the Sedition Act of 1798, Federalists used prosecutions in the federal courts to silence political opposition, and in 1801 the Federalist majority in Congress expanded federal jurisdiction at the expense of state courts and created new courts with additional judgeships that were filled by the lame-duck President, John Adams. Republicans came into power soon thereafter determined to curb what they saw as the partisan bias of federal judges. The Republican Congress abolished the new courts and judgeships and impeached two highly partisan judges. Republicans argued that the Constitution granted Congress full authority to establish the judicial system and that the constitutional protections of tenure during good behavior and undiminished salary did not prevent Congress from abolishing courts that were no longer needed. Republicans also argued that the partisan actions of Federalist judges, particularly in the Sedition Act prosecutions, had undermined all pretense of impartiality and judicial independence. Federalists meanwhile decried what they saw as an assault on the constitutional guarantee of tenure during good behavior. The Constitution, they declared, made the judges independent so as "to control the fiery zeal, and to quell the fierce passions" of a newly elected party. Repeal of the Judiciary Act of 1801 and the precedent of depriving judges of their office, Federalists warned, would render all judges the tools of political parties and bring about the collapse of constitutional government.

Despite the private doubts of Chief Justice John Marshall and other justices, the Supreme Court in 1803 issued a decision that let stand the law abolishing the courts and judgeships established in 1801. Republican fears about the judiciary were heightened, however, by the Supreme Court's decision one week earlier, in which Chief Justice Marshall, in *Marbury v. Madison,* asserted the judiciary's right to declare an act of Congress unconstitutional and, more alarming to Republicans, the Court's authority to compel executive compliance with an act of Congress. After the Senate failed to convict Supreme Court Justice Samuel Chase in his impeachment trial of 1805, a truce of sorts fell into place as Republicans abandoned their impeachment plans and the most overtly partisan Federalist judges, like Chase, curtailed their political activity. The temporary lull in public debates, however, did not signify a consensus on the proper measure of judicial independence.

Throughout the early decades of the nineteenth century, unpopular decisions in the Supreme Court and, more often, in the federal trial courts, sparked recurring demands for restricting judicial tenure or limiting federal jurisdiction. Thomas Jefferson, as President and during his long retirement, advocated fixed, renewable terms of office for federal judges. Jefferson asserted that with impeachment the only means of removal, the judges "consider themselves secure for life; they skulk from responsibility to public opinion." Members of Congress and the majorities of several state legislatures repeatedly called for restrictions on the authority of federal courts to review the decisions of state courts or an end to federal jurisdiction over suits between residents of different states. Others submitted amendments to allow for the removal of judges on the vote of supermajorities in Congress or to place age limits on judicial service. None of these proposals succeeded, but their introduction into nearly every Congress before the Civil War indicated that judicial independence remained a subject of political debate.

4. An Independent Judiciary in a Reconstructed Union

The crisis of union surrounding the Civil War brought new challenges to judicial independence. Unionists and supporters of the anti-slavery movement were highly suspicious of the federal courts because of decisions in support of slavery and particularly because of the Supreme Court's 1857 *Dred Scott* decision, which, among other things, denied all African Americans any rights under the Constitution. Following the close of the Civil War, Republicans in Congress feared that the federal courts would disallow much of their ambitious legislation designed to ensure full citizenship rights for freed slaves and all other African Americans. Congress debated numerous proposals to strip the federal courts of specific jurisdiction and to reorganize the courts. Congress redrew circuit boundaries to ensure that Southern states would no longer hold a majority of seats on the Supreme Court. In 1868, the Congress repealed the Supreme Court's jurisdiction over appeals of habeas corpus petitions, thus preventing former Confederates from challenging the custody of military courts. The House of Representatives in

1868 approved legislation that would have required a majority of seven justices for the Supreme Court to disallow any congressional statute, although the Senate Committee on the Judiciary failed to report the bill.

The willingness of Congress to reorganize the judiciary and to restrict jurisdiction in pursuit of the goals of Reconstruction was counter-balanced by the congressional Republicans' reliance on the federal courts to enforce federal law in the former Confederate states. In 1869, Congress established nine circuit judgeships in the hope, as expressed by Senator Lyman Trumbull, that "nothing would do more to give quiet and peace to the southern country than an efficient enforcement of the laws of the United States in the United States courts." In 1875, Congress extended federal jurisdiction to encompass all cases arising under the Constitution and federal law, so that by the close of Reconstruction in 1877 the federal courts had unprecedented authority and independence.

5.   The Federal Courts and the Politics of an Industrial United States

The most sustained effort to make federal judges more directly accountable to public opinion and to the elected branches of government arose between the 1890s and the 1920s when the federal courts became involved in labor struggles and in debates over government regulation of the economy. The federal courts' approval of injunctions to halt labor strikes and the Supreme Court's disallowance of regulatory legislation contributed to support for various restrictions on judicial authority. Populists seeking to regulate railroad shipping rates, labor unions trying to establish the right to strike, and Progressives defending their extensive program of social welfare and regulation of corporations all in turn advocated legislation to restrict the jurisdiction of the federal courts or to make judges more responsive to shifts in public opinion. The most common proposals included the election of federal judges, fixed judicial terms, narrow limits on federal jurisdiction, and the abolition of judicial review or requirements for a super-majority of the Supreme Court to invalidate federal or state laws. For nearly thirty years, Justice Walter Clark of the North Carolina Supreme Court cultivated national support for the election of federal judges and limits on judicial review. Senator George Norris of Nebraska personally favored the abolition of the lower federal courts and introduced more widely supported bills to restrict judicial review, impose fixed terms on judges, and strip the courts of authority to issue labor injunctions. In 1924, Senator Robert LaFollette, the Progressive Party candidate for President, proposed a constitutional amendment that would have prohibited the lower federal courts from invalidating any congressional statute and would also have authorized Congress to reenact any legislation overturned by the Supreme Court.

Although the House of Representatives Committee on the Judiciary in 1894 reported a bill to limit judges to 10-year terms, few of the proposals to limit judicial independence gained much ground in Congress over the next 40 years, and the diverse critics of the courts never unified behind a common program. The critique of the federal courts, however, was steady and became an important part of the broader public debates on the effectiveness of government in a time of rapid social and economic change. The proposals to limit the authority of the federal judiciary paralleled the movement in the states to subject local judges to recall by popular vote.

Throughout the early decades of the twentieth century, the defense of the existing judicial system was led by the organized bar, especially the American Bar Association. Defenders of tenure during good behavior and judicial review warned that a judiciary beholden to public opinion would never be able to protect civil liberties and economic rights. William Howard Taft, as President, then as dean of Yale Law School, and after 1921 as Chief Justice of the United States, was an important advocate for the established protections of judicial independence. Taft conceded that the federal courts would always be subject to popular criticism because their role was to protect "the guaranties of personal liberty . . . against the partisan zeal of the then majority."

6. "Court Packing" and the Defense of Judicial Independence

After several years of Supreme Court decisions that challenged key New Deal programs, President Franklin Roosevelt in 1937 proposed a sweeping change in the appointment of all federal judges. Never in United States history had a proposal about the judiciary excited such political debate. The Judicial Reorganization bill would have authorized the President to appoint an additional judge whenever a sitting judge on any federal court did not retire within six months of reaching the age of 70. If approved, the bill would have allowed Roosevelt to appoint immediately as many as 50 new federal judges, including six Supreme Court justices. Roosevelt alleged that the declining abilities of aging judges contributed to a backlog of cases, but he also argued that a regular appointment of new judges was necessary "to bring to the decision of social and economic problems younger men who have had personal experience and contact with modern facts and circumstances under which average men have to live and work."

For months, the judiciary proposal dominated public debate throughout the nation. While many New Dealers supported the bill, defections from

Roosevelt's own party doomed the legislation and led the Senate Committee on the Judiciary to recommend that the bill not pass. The Senate committee report described the bill as "an invasion of judicial power such as has never been attempted in this country" and warned that the bill would set a dangerous precedent allowing a Congress or a President to impose constitutional beliefs on the courts. While some attributed the lack of support to the Supreme Court's recent willingness to uphold New Deal legislation (the so-called "switch in time that saved nine"), the opposition to Roosevelt's bill rested on fundamental beliefs about the independence of the judiciary. Roosevelt had clearly challenged a widely shared, popular commitment to the balance of power between the branches of government. Even older Progressives who had supported limited tenure for judges and restrictions on federal jurisdiction shied away from what they saw as Roosevelt's attempted power grab for the executive branch. The administration drafted a revised bill, but that too met with opposition, and the Senate never voted on it. The retirement of Supreme Court justices soon gave Roosevelt the opportunity to appoint a majority of that court, but the court-packing crisis in many ways strengthened support for an independent judiciary and discouraged further proposals for any comprehensive reorganization of the judiciary.

7.   The Persistence of Court Critics

Despite greater public acknowledgment of the principle of judicial independence in the years following the New Deal, critics of federal court decisions continued to call for limits on federal jurisdiction or for changes in judicial tenure. In the 1950s, in response to *Brown v. Board of Education* and subsequent court enforcement of school desegregation, segregationists advocated various measures to deprive federal courts of jurisdiction over issues related to local schools. In the 1960s, a series of Supreme Court decisions on the rights of criminal defendants, school prayer, and reapportionment of congressional seats fueled a campaign to impeach Chief Justice Earl Warren. To this day, controversial court decisions are often followed by proposals to "strip" the federal courts of specific jurisdiction or even challenges to judicial tenure during good behavior. Like similar proposals dating back 200 years, few have gained serious congressional consideration.

8.   Institutionalization of Judicial Independence

Over the course of the twentieth century, judicial independence was greatly strengthened by the development of institutions for the federal courts' self governance. In an address to the American Bar Association in 1914, William Howard Taft recognized that widespread public criticism of the courts imposed on judges and lawyers the responsibility to ensure a court system worthy of public respect. Taft became a leader in the development of institutions that have allowed the judiciary to govern itself and to guarantee the public a fair and efficient system of justice. Through much of the country's history, the courts received administrative support from various departments of the executive branch. Taft's support for the establishment in 1922 of a conference of chief judges from each circuit was the first step toward independent judicial administration. In 1939, Congress established the Administrative Office of the U.S. Courts, which reported to the conference of judges and provided courts with the support formerly given by the Department of Justice. The congressional act of 1939 also established in each circuit judicial councils with responsibility for improving the administration of all courts within the circuit. The establishment of the Federal Judicial Center in 1967 gave the federal courts their own agency for education of judges and court staff and for research on improving judicial administration.

9. Public Trust

As Taft recognized in the early decades of the twentieth century, the independence of the judiciary depends not only on the constitutional protections of judges, but also on public faith in a fair and responsive court system. The debates on Roosevelt's court-packing plan revealed that public trust in the judiciary was also based on confidence that the federal courts would not be dominated by another branch of government or by one political party. Critics of judicial independence have always been part of political life in the United States, but in the 200 years following the debates between Federalists and Republicans, the changing majorities in Congress have been reluctant to endorse sweeping changes in the federal judiciary, especially in response to specific court decisions or to further partisan policy.

Part II. Judicial Independence and the Federal Courts— Suggested Discussion Topics

1. Alexander Hamilton argued that the success of constitutional government depended on a judiciary free from the influence of sudden shifts in public opinion. What dangers did Hamilton perceive in a judiciary subject to popular politics? Has the subsequent history of political debates on the judiciary confirmed or challenged Hamilton's argument?

   Related documents: 1, 4, 5, 6, 8, 10

2. The Constitution grants Congress the authority to establish federal courts in addition to the Supreme Court and to determine most of the jurisdiction of all federal courts. Over the course of the nation's history, what kinds of congressional legislation related to the courts were considered a proper exercise of constitutional authority and what kinds of legislation were considered an improper interference with judicial independence?

   Related documents: 3, 4, 6, 7, 9, 10

3. Representative Joseph Nicholson and former President Thomas Jefferson warned that a judiciary "beyond the control" or "independent" of the nation was a threat to a republican system of government. "Brutus" had expressed similar concerns during the ratification debates. What dangers did they see? How might defenders of the constitutional protections of judicial independence, from Alexander Hamilton to the Senate Committee on the Judiciary in 1937, have responded?

   Related documents: 1, 2, 3, 4, 5, 8, 10

4. The rise of political parties in the late 1790s led to the first great debates on judicial independence. How did the contest between political parties threaten the constitutional provisions for judicial independence? What later party struggles challenged judicial independence?

   Related documents: 3, 4, 8, 9, 10

5. William Howard Taft strongly defended the constitutional protections of judicial independence, but he also believed judges were responsible for maintaining public respect for the federal judiciary. How did Taft hope to ensure public trust in the judiciary? Throughout the nation's history, what has contributed to popular respect for and faith in the federal court system?

   Related documents: 7, 8, 4, 10

6. When Franklin Roosevelt proposed to authorize the appointment of additional judges when sitting judges reached the age of 70, he provoked intense opposition, even from within his own party and from many who had advocated limited terms of office for judges. What explains the strength of the opposition to Roosevelt's "court-packing" plan? How did the plan challenge popular beliefs about judicial independence?

Related documents: 9, 10

Part III.   Judicial Independence and the Federal Courts— Historical Documents

1.   Alexander Hamilton, The Federalist No. 78

If then the courts of justice are to be considered as the bulwarks of a limited constitution against legislative encroachments, this consideration will afford a strong argument for the permanent tenure of judicial offices, since nothing will contribute so much as this to that independent spirit in the judges, which must be essential to the faithful performance of so arduous a duty.

This independence of the judges is equally requisite to guard the constitution and the rights of individuals from the effects of those ill humours which the arts of designing men, or the influence of particular conjunctures, sometimes disseminate among the people themselves, and which, though they speedily give place to better information and more deliberate reflection, have a tendency in the mean time to occasion dangerous innovations in the government, and serious oppressions of the minor party in the community.

. . . That inflexible and uniform adherence to the rights of the constitution and of individuals, which we perceive to be indispensable in the courts of justice, can certainly not be expected from judges who hold their offices by a temporary commission. Periodical appointments, however regulated, or by whomsoever made, would in some way or other be fatal to their necessary independence. If the power of making them was committed either to the executive or legislature, there would be danger of an improper complaisance to the branch which possessed it; if to both, there would be an unwillingness to hazard the displeasure of either; if to the people, or to persons chosen by them for the special purpose, there would be too great a disposition to consult popularity, to justify a reliance that nothing would be consulted but the constitution and the laws.

[Document Source: *The Debate on the Constitution*, ed. Bailyn, 471–74.]

2.   Letters of "Brutus," XV

The judges in England are under the controul of the legislature, for they are bound to determine according to the laws passed by them. But the judges under this constitution will controul the legislature, for the supreme court are authorised in the last resort, to determine what is the extent of the powers of the Congress; they are to give the constitution an explanation, and there is no power above them to sit aside their judgment. The framers of this constitution appear to have followed that of the British, in rendering the judges independent, by granting them their offices during good behaviour, without following the constitution of England, in instituting a tribunal in which their errors may be corrected; and without adverting to this, that the judicial under this system have a power which is above the legislative, and which indeed transcends any power given to a judicial by any free government under heaven.

I do not object to the judges holding their commissions during good behaviour. I suppose it a proper provision provided they were made properly responsible. But I say, this system has followed the English government in this, while it has departed from almost every other principle of their jurisprudence, under the idea, of rendering the judges independent; which, in the British constitution, means no more than that they hold their places during good behaviour, and have fixed salaries, they have made the judges *independent*, in the fullest sense of the word. There is no power above them, to controul any of their decisions. There is no authority that can remove them, and they cannot be controuled by the laws of the legislature. In short, they are independent of the people, of the legislature, and of every power under heaven. Men placed in this situation will generally soon feel themselves independent of heaven itself.

[Document Source: *The Debate on the Constitution*, ed. Bailyn, 372–78.]

3. Joseph Nicholson on Repeal of the Judiciary Act of 1801

Our doctrine is, that every Congress has a right to repeal any law passed by its predecessors, except in cases where the Constitution imposes a prohibition. We have been told that we cannot repeal a law fixing the President's salary, during the period for which he was elected. This is admitted, because it is so expressly declared in the Constitution; nor is the necessity so imperious, because, at the expiration of every four years, it is in the power of Congress to regulate it anew, as their judgments may dictate. Neither can we diminish the salary of a judge so long as he continues in office, because in this particular the Constitution is express likewise; but we do contend that we have an absolute, uncontrolled right to abolish all offices, which have been created by Congress, when in our judgment those offices are unnecessary, and are productive of a useless expense.

. . . If the feelings and interests of the nation require that new laws should be enacted, that existing laws should be modified, or that useless and unnecessary laws should be repealed, they [the people] have reserved this power to themselves by declaring that it should be exercised by persons freely chosen for a limited period to represent them in the National Legislature. On what ground is it denied to them in the present instance? By what authority are the judges to be raised above the law and above the Constitution? Where is the charter which places the sovereignty of this country in their hands? Give them the powers and the independence now contended for, and they will require nothing more; for your Government becomes a despotism, and they become your rulers. They are to decide upon the lives, the liberties, and the property of your citizens; they have an absolute veto upon your laws by declaring them null and void at pleasure; they are to introduce at will the laws of a foreign country, differing essentially with us upon the great principles of government; and after being clothed with this arbitrary power, they are beyond the control of the nation, as they are not to be affected by any laws which the people by their representatives can pass. If all this be true; if this doctrine be established in the extent which is now contended for, the Constitution is not worth the time we are spending upon it. It is, as it has been called by its enemies, mere parchment. For these judges, thus rendered omnipotent, may overlap the Constitution and trample on your laws; they may laugh the Legislature to scorn, and set the nation at defiance.

[Document Source: *Annals of Congress*, 7th Cong., 1st sess., 818, 823–24.]

4. James A. Bayard on Repeal of the Judiciary Act of 1801

Let me now suppose, that in our frame of government the judges are a check upon the Legislature; that the Constitution is deposited in their keeping. Will you say afterwards that their existence depends upon the Legislature? . . . A check must necessarily imply a power commensurate to its end. The political body designed to check another must be independent of it, otherwise there can be no check. What check can there be when the power designed to be checked can annihilate the body which is to restrain it?

. . . If your judges are independent of political changes, they may have their preferences, but they will not enter into the spirit of party. But let their existence depend upon the support of the power of a certain set of men and they cannot be impartial. Justice will be trodden under foot. Your courts will lose all public confidence and respect. The judges will be supported by their partisans, who in their turn will expect impunity for the wrongs and violence they commit. The spirit of party will be inflamed to madness; and the moment is not far off when this fair country is to be desolated by civil war.

. . . The independence of the Judiciary was the felicity of our Constitution. It was this principle which was to curb the fury of party upon sudden changes. The first moments of power, gained by a struggle, are the most vindictive and intemperate. Raised above the storm, it was the Judiciary which was to control the fiery zeal, and to quell the fierce passions of a victorious faction.

[Document Source: *Annals of Congress*, 7th Cong., 1st sess., 648–50.]

5. Thomas Jefferson to James Pleasants, December 26, 1821

A better remedy I think, and indeed the best I can devise would be to give future commissions to judges for six years (the Senatorial term) with a reappoint-mentability by the president with the approbation of <u>both</u> houses. That of the H. of Repr. imports a majority of citizens, that of the Senate a majority of states, and that of both a majority of the three sovereign departments of the existing government, to wit, of it's Executive & legislative branches. If this would not be independence enough, I know not what would be such, short of the total irresponsibility under which they are acting and sinning now. The independence of the judges in England on the King alone is good; but even there they are not independent on the Parliament; being removable on the joint address of both houses by a vote of a majority of each, but we require a majority of one house and 2/3 of the other, a concurrence which, in practice, has been and ever will be found impossible; for the judiciary perversions of the constitution will forever be protested under the pretext of errors of judgment, which by principle, are exempt from punishment. Impeachment therefore is a bug bear which they fear not at all. But they would be under some awe of the canvas of their conduct which would be open to both houses regularly every 6th year. It is a misnomer to call a government republican, in which a branch of the supreme power is independent of the nation.

[Document Source: The Thomas Jefferson Papers, Series I, General Correspondence, 1651–1827, Library of Congress Manuscripts Division. (Available at http://memory.loc.gov/ammem/index.html)]

6. In Support of an Elected Federal Judiciary, by Walter Clark, North Carolina
    Supreme Court, 1903

Probably the most serious defect in the Federal Constitution is the retention unaltered of the mode for the selection of the Federal judges at third hand through the instrumentality of the Executive and the Senate, and for life. In truth no provision could be more undemocratic than the manner of selecting these important officials and their life tenure. They are chosen in a manner that entirely negatives any expression of public opinion, and that permits their selection by powerful influences that usually have ready access to the appointing power. This is an anomaly in a country whose government is based upon the principle that it exists only by the consent of the governed. The power that has been assumed and maintained by the judiciary to set aside the action of the legislative and executive departments was unknown when the Constitution was adopted, and it has become vitally necessary, if such power shall remain, as is probable, in the judiciary, that the judiciary shall at least be selected by the same element that chooses the Federal legislature; otherwise the will of the people is at the mercy of officials who are under no control and are not selected by the popular will. It is due mainly to the high personal character of most of the gentlemen who have occupied the Federal bench that this anachronism has not met with a stronger and more universal demand for its removal. The fact that nearly every State in the Union has made its judiciary elective by the people proves that the mature judgment and the deliberate will of the people of the United States upon this subject are well-nigh overwhelming.

[Document Source: Walter Clark, "Law and Human Progress," *American Law Review* 37 (1903): 512–29.]

7. William Howard Taft, Address to the American Bar Association, 1914

The agitation with reference to the courts, the general attacks upon them, the grotesque remedies proposed of recall of judges and recall of judicial decisions, and the resort of demagogues to the unpopularity of courts as a means of promoting their own political fortunes, all impose upon us, members of the Bar and upon judges of the courts and legislatures, the duty to remove, as far as possible, grounds for just criticism of our judicial system. The federal system extends into every state. It is under the control of one legislature and subordinate to one Supreme Court. Here is the opportunity to furnish to the country a model which shall inspire state legislatures and state Supreme Courts to similar efforts to make their courts the handmaid of prompt justice.

[Document Source: Report of the Thirty-seventh Annual Meeting of the American Bar Association, Baltimore: Lord Baltimore Press, 1914, 359–84.]

8. William Howard Taft on Judicial Independence, 1923

From time to time, by reason of its jurisdiction and a proper exercise of it, the Court can not help becoming the stormy petrel of politics. It is the head of the system of Federal Courts established avowedly to avoid the local prejudice which non-residents may encounter in State Courts, a function often likely to ruffle the sensibilities of the communities, the possibility of whose prejudice is thus recognized and avoided. More than this, the Court's duty to ignore the acts of Congress or of the State Legislatures, if out of line with the fundamental law of the Nation, inevitably throws it as an obstruction across the path of the then majority who have enacted the invalid legislation. The stronger the majority, and the more intense its partisan feeling, the less likely is it to regard constitutional limitations upon its power, and the more likely is it to enact laws of questionable validity. It is convincing evidence of the sound sense of the American People in the long run and their love of civil liberty and its constitutional guaranties, that, in spite of hostility thus frequently engendered, the Court has lived with its powers unimpaired until the present day.

[Document Source: "Dedication of Memorial to Chief Justice Salmon Portland Chase," *American Bar Association Journal*, 9 (1923): 347–52.]

9. President Franklin D. Roosevelt, Message to Congress presenting a plan for the Reorganization of the Judicial Branch of Government, February 5, 1937

Modern complexities call also for a constant infusion of new blood in the courts, just as it is needed in executive functions of the Government and in private business. A lowered mental or physical vigor leads men to avoid an examination of complicated and changed conditions. Little by little, new facts become blurred through old glasses fitted, as it were, for the needs of another generation; older men, assuming that the scene is the same as it was in the past, cease to explore or inquire into the present or the future.

. . . Life tenure of judges, assured by the Constitution, was designed to place the courts beyond temptations or influences which might impair their judgments: it was not intended to create a static judiciary. A constant and systematic addition of younger blood will vitalize the courts and better equip them to recognize and apply the essential concepts of justice in the light of the needs and the facts of an everchanging world.

It is obvious, therefore, from both reason and experience, that some provision must be adopted, which will operate automatically to supplement the work of older judges and accelerate the work of the court.

I, therefore, earnestly recommend that the necessity of an increase in the number of judges be supplied by legislation providing for the appointment of additional judges in all federal courts, without exception, where there are incumbent judges of retirement age who do not choose to retire or to resign. If an elder judge is not in fact incapacitated, only good can come from the presence of an additional judge in the crowded state of the dockets; if the capacity of an elder judge is in fact impaired, the appointment of an additional judge is indispensable.

[Document Source: The Public Papers and Addresses of Franklin D. Roosevelt. 1937 Volume: The Constitution Prevails. New York: Macmillan Company, 1941, 51–66.]

10. Senate Judiciary Committee, Adverse Report on Roosevelt's Proposed Reorganization of the Federal Judiciary, June 1937

It is essential to the continuance of our constitutional democracy that the judiciary be completely independent of both the executive and legislative branches of the

Government, and we assert that independent courts are the last safeguard of the citizen, where his rights, reserved to him by the express and implied provisions of the Constitution, come in conflict with the power of governmental agencies. . . .

The condition of the world abroad must of necessity cause us to hesitate at this time and to refuse to enact any law that would impair the independence of or destroy the people's confidence in an independent judicial branch of our Government. We unhesitatingly assert that any effort looking to the impairment of an independent judiciary of necessity operates toward centralization of power in the other branches of a tripartite form of government. We declare for the continuance and perpetuation of government and rule by law, as distinguished from government and rule by men, and in this we are but reasserting the principles basic to the Constitution of the United States. . . .

The whole bill prophesies and permits executive and legislative interferences with the independence of the Court, a prophecy and a permission which constitute an affront to the spirit of the Constitution. . . .

If interference with the judgment of an independent judiciary is to be countenanced in any degree, then it is permitted and sanctioned in all degrees. There is no constituted power to say where the degree ends or begins, and the political administration of the hour may apply the essential "concepts of justice" by equipping the courts with one strain of "new blood," while the political administration of another day may use a different light and a different blood test. Thus would influence run riot. Thus perpetuity, independence, and stability belonging to the judicial arm of the Government and relied on by lawyers and laity, are lost. Thus is confidence extinguished.

[Document Source: Senate Committee on the Judiciary, Reorganization of the Federal Judiciary, 75th Cong., 1st sess., 1937, S. Rep. 711.]

Bibliography

The Debate on the Constitution: Federalist and Anti-Federalist Speeches, Articles, and Letters During the Struggle over Ratification. Bernard Bailyn, ed. 2 vols. New York: Library of America, 1993.

Geyh, Charles Gardner. *When Courts and Congress Collide: The Struggle for Control of America's Judicial System*. Ann Arbor: University of Michigan Press, 2006.

Ross, William G. *A Muted Fury: Populists, Progressives, and Labor Unions confront the Courts, 1890-1937*. Princeton, N.J.: Princeton University Press, 1994.